Pancakes

Written by Sandra Iversen • Illustrated by Pat Reynolds

"Please get me the flour, Jimmy," said Gran.
Jimmy got the flour for Gran.

2

"Please get me the eggs,
Jimmy," said Gran.
Jimmy got the eggs for Gran.

3

"Please get me the milk,
Jimmy," said Gran.
Jimmy got the milk for Gran.

4

"Please get me the wooden spoon,
Jimmy," said Gran.
Jimmy got the wooden spoon for Gran.

5

Gran mixed the flour
and the eggs and the milk
and put them in the pan.

6

"Now for the fun!"
said Gran.
She flipped the pancake.
It went up and over,
and it came down into the pan.

7

"Flip the pancake, Jimmy,"
said Gran.
Jimmy tried to flip the pancake.
The pancake did not go up.
It stayed in the pan.

8

"Try again, Jimmy,"
said Gran.
Jimmy tried to flip the pancake again.
The pancake went up and down
into the pan.

9

"Try again, Jimmy," said Gran.
Jimmy flipped the pancake.
The pancake went up and over
and down into the pan.

10

"Good!" said Gran.
"Please get me the syrup, Jimmy,"
said Gran.
Jimmy got the syrup.

11

Jimmy and Gran ate the pancake.